M000192023

BEHIND THE CURTAIN

An Inclusive and Observational Reconciliation of
Quantum Physics and Religion

FRANK PATRICK

Copyright © 2022 Frank Patrick

All rights reserved. No part of this publication in print or in electronic format may be reproduced, stored in a retrieval system, or transmitted in any form or by any means, electronic, mechanical, photocopying, recording, or otherwise without the prior written permission of the publisher.

The scanning, uploading, and distribution of this book without permission is a theft of the author's intellectual property. Thank you for your support of the author's rights.

Editing, design, and distribution by Bublish, Inc.

ISBN: 978-1-647045-52-4 (eBook)
ISBN: 978-1-647045-53-1 (paperback)

CONTENTS

PREFACE

For millennia, civilizations have understandably gravitated toward and organized around religion as a means to diminish chaos, connect with divine energy, and build societies. In this way, science has finally caught up with religion.

As Elon Musk said, "Engineering is the closest thing to magic that exists in the world."

For example, do you know how a speaker works? Compressed air molecules called "sound" create electromagnetic waves in the air that are sensed by a copper-wire coil and then conducted to another copper-wire coil that is surrounded by a circular magnet in the speaker. The copper wire emits the sound because a circular magnet quantumly extracts the electromagnetic wave that carries the information of the original sound from the wire to create an interference pattern in the molecules we call sound. The sound is then intensified in the speaker cone by making the cone vibrate, thus pushing the sound toward the listener. So, it is the electromagnetic waves in the copper wire that emit the sound. Yes, you read that correctly. The sound comes directly out of the wire.

Is that magic or not?

Most people do not know how a speaker works. Nor do they understand the physics that makes most modern-day devices work.

This book bridges quantum physics, psychology, and science with religion.

What did Jesus mean when he said in the Bible, "The thought is as bad as the act"? What did he mean when he said to his followers, "When you do this to the least of my brothers, you have done it unto me"?

This book explains what he meant, not just figuratively but literally.

For science now harnesses the magic of the universe and explains the divine energy creating it. The problem is that religions often discount science, and scientists typically discount religion. So, the two have remained in their respective silos. At the peak of technological advancement, which we are near, it takes someone fascinated with both religion and science to reconcile both.

I would like to be that someone.

So, why did I decide to write this book? What do I know about awareness, science, and religion? What do I know about bringing them together in a way that is inclusive and objective? Why would I write a book designing a measurable and predictable path to success?

I was born disadvantaged. I had many obstacles to overcome. However, I was also blessed. I had a wonderful childhood. Growing up in south St. Louis, I was part of a large but less-than-traditional family. I had three fathers. I had a biological father whom I met twice. I had a stepfather who was the nuts and bolts of our family and my upbringing. Then, I had another father who seemed to come out of nowhere, but he was an absolute godsend.

Since I was a child, I've always been fascinated with both science and religion. I grew up in a Catholic/Christian family. I went to a Catholic grade school and high school. Both the Old and the New Testaments were a large part of my life for many years. I enjoyed being a student, especially of the New Testament and, even more specifically, of the Sermon on the Mount. Later in life, I desired clearer answers to questions regarding God, life, death, and the human experience. I turned my attention elsewhere and became a student of science. Specifically, I became a student of Newtonian physics and quantum physics. I also studied religions and philosophies other than my own. I was, and still am, a big fan of James Redfield and Neale Donald Walsch, and I consider these two authors thought leaders in spirituality.

Thanks to some fabulous parents and my own grit, I had become as holistic as I could possibly be. I found myself in an all-male Catholic military high school in Clayton, Missouri. While there, I played varsity football. I was a straight-A student. That landed me in a six-year medical program at a university in Kansas City, Missouri. After six years, I moved back to my hometown and participated in a four-year obstetrical-gynecological residency program. Next, I joined a practice in St. Louis County, where I went on to deliver more than six thousand babies before I turned fifty. During that time, I felt at times to be an amateur business owner, accountant, attorney, psychologist, road and off-road biker, and even beer league ice hockey player. I was successful, but I also made mistakes. I did brilliant things. I did stupid things. I managed life crises. I experienced myself as a gritty and disciplined human. However, I also experienced myself as careless. I learned that awareness did not mean perfection. Ouch!

Since my early teens, I've made it a priority to be whole and to experience myself as holistically as possible. I made a list of boxes to be checked off to mark my progress toward being and experiencing as many parts of who I am as I imagined existed. Then, I checked them off. After gaining these experiences, I wrote this book.

This book explains in detail the definition, purpose, structure, and function of the observable universe as it relates to religious dogma and spirituality.

After all these years, science has caught up to religion in terms of explaining the big picture. Furthermore, it does so not just by explaining who, what, where, and when, but also by explaining why.

Isaac Newton said that he could see further because he was standing on the shoulders of giants. The information contained in this narrative is intended to act in this manner as well. Inclusive observations discussed in this book have been extracted from science, religion, thought leaders, and my own experience. I would like to think of this book as the result of a lifetime of observing the cream of the crop in religion, science, philosophy, and psychology.

The purpose of this book is to birth awareness of core realities with the intention of bringing actionable solutions resulting in the diminishment of the mundane, unknown, and unwelcome life states and situations that can cause anxiety, depression, confusion, insecurity, and suffering. At the same time, these actionable solutions will foster joy, happiness, and love. I hope for the melding of science and religion in this book to be simpler, quicker, and more efficient than prior respectable narrations.

Another distinction would be that this book does not rely on revelation but is instead based on observation. Furthermore, this book is inclusive, not exclusive. Whether you believe in science, religion, spirituality, or God, the inclusive and objective observations regarding the best of what science and religion have to offer will work in a predictable and measurable fashion for any reader regardless of their background, perspective, culture, or upbringing. This is because objective and inclusive observations are readily discernible to any individual.

1

AWARENESS

Science without religion is lame, religion without science is blind.

—*Albert Einstein*

Anxiety, depression, confusion, insecurity, and suffering are most effectively dissipated with awareness. Happiness, joy, creativity, excitement, and security are most effectively realized with awareness. It has been said that the pinnacle of success is being able to create and experience your desires with effortless ease. While that is a high bar to achieve, it is not a bad goal. If this goal is achievable, awareness is the path to it.

People struggle with making decisions regarding the external environment, including those related to life, science, religion, and spirituality. Recent examples include the COVID-19 pandemic. "Do I get the vaccine, or do I not get the vaccine?" "Do I wear a mask, or do I not wear a mask?" "Should I go to church, or should I not go to church?" "Do I do what others want me to do, or do I do what I want to do?"

Being aware is like turning on a light bulb in a dark room. Awareness is essential to answering questions like these in a way that allows you to be successful. At every point in your existence, you will have a choice. Choices made in awareness can lead to happiness, joy, creativity, excitement, and security. Choices made in a lack of awareness are more likely to lead to anxiety, depression, confusion, insecurity, and suffering.

Awareness is a skeleton key. It is a silver bullet. Awareness is enlightenment. It is nirvana. It is what everyone is seeking—consciously or subconsciously.

You may ask, "But awareness of what?"

Awareness of the only thing that matters. And the only thing that matters is God's dilemma, which is **eternity**.

That may sound too simple. But imagine, if you will, how long eternity is. Furthermore, eternity *has* to exist because there can't be something before or after eternity. That logic breaks down even further because if there is no beginning, then there is no end. Most people who believe in God agree that God is eternal.

Eternity is an exceedingly long time. And if God is conscious, then God has to deal with this amount of time. It's as simple as that. But worry not; God, of course, developed a solution. God's solution to dealing with the dilemma of eternity has been elucidated by scientists, religions, and thought leaders. **An objective interpretation of science and religion yields the framework of God's solution.**

Unfortunately, most solutions of God have been proposed via religions based on revelation and exclusion. But this book is based on observation, not revelation. One can agree or disagree with the accuracy of the observations. Also, there are times when the observations have a trajectory. Generally speaking, an idea of God based on observation instead of revelation is a new concept.

Religions are respectable and honorable. Religions call upon people to be their absolute best. However, religions are based on revelation, and revelation cannot be dependable. If revelation were dependable, there would not be so many religions and so many conflicts.

Religions are not inclusive. Some religions even believe that if you don't agree with them, God will punish you for an eternity in a fiery hell. Now that's exclusion! But the unifying theory contained in this book, which brings science and religion together, is inclusive. It includes the believer and the nonbeliever; it includes the Jew and the Hindu. No one is discounted.

So, back to God's solution. What did God come up with that could possibly preoccupy such an enormous consciousness for an eternity? The truth is, God only thought of three things. They play continuously on a never-ending loop. God invented the **human soul**, which engages in the process of **life** and continually renews itself through **death**. The understanding of these three elements from an inclusive and observational perspective is how God solved the problem of being an eternal being.

As noted, prior attempts to explain God, the human soul, life, and death have been based more on revelation than on observation. But by cherry-picking the conclusions of our best scientists and most notable religions, we can be more specific in detailing the definitions, purposes, structures, and functions of God, life, the human soul, and even the process of death. By making objective and inclusive observations, these mysteries can be elucidated. Then, suddenly, eternity becomes fun!

2

GOD

I want to know God's thoughts; the rest are details.
—Albert Einstein to student Esther Salaman, 1925

Just as Einstein sought to understand the large cosmic processes, I was taught as a medical student to understand the human body.

For instance, medical students are taught complex human organ systems in an organized yet separate fashion. The definition, purpose, structure, and function of each organ system is discussed in detail to give the medical student a full understanding of how each system works in the human body.

So, in this book, we are going to discuss how God, the human soul, life, and death serve to eliminate God's dilemma of getting bored with eternity. The awareness of the definition, purpose, structure, and function of each of these four subjects would indeed cause eternity to be far less boring. In fact, once understood, eternity is no longer God's dilemma; eternity becomes God's blessing.

As we observe the great accomplishments of scientists, religions, and thought leaders, we will proceed with the definition, purpose, structure, and function of God in an observational and all-inclusive description.

THE DEFINITION OF GOD

I have heard it said that if you blow up a junkyard and, at the end of the explosion, when all of the debris has settled, you find a functioning Boeing 747 airplane, then a miracle has occurred. There are no strings of coincidences that can lead to such an outcome.

Similarly, if you listen to a song, understand how the most advanced technology works, or simply look in the eyes of your own child, it is hard to imagine that the universe is a petri dish with a very unlikely, intricate, random, chemical outcome.

As I will describe shortly, it is science that proves there is a God. But until I get to the scientific experiments that led to this planet-changing discovery, let us say that the definition of God is the projection of space, time, matter, and energy from a limitless source of intelligence.

THE PURPOSE OF GOD

The universe, solar system, and life have all been created. Life creates itself repeatedly. It is safe to say that **the purpose of God is creation**.

If you look at the process of creation from the perspective of the human experience as well as from your own experience, you can easily see that it is a circle. **The circle starts with intention.** You can be aware of your intentions or unaware of your intentions. If you are unaware of your intentions, your process of creation will not work. If you are aware of your intentions, your process of creation will work. Choose awareness of your intentions. **Intentions have perspective.** Perspective comes from love or from fear. Choose love. **Perspective**

leads to thoughts. Thoughts can be pleasurable. Thoughts can be unpleasurable. Choose pleasurable. **Thoughts lead to words.** Words can be empowering or disempowering. Choose empowering. Whether they are spoken or kept in your head, words can be uplifting or deflating. Choose uplifting. **Words lead to actions.** Actions are either purposeful or random and chaotic. Choose purposeful. **Actions lead to experience.** The experience either works or it does not. By "working," I mean the intended experience is manifested. If an experience works, then that experience is in line with your original intention. If an experience does not work, it is not in line with your original intention. Finally, **experience leads to observation.** The observation of your own experience is either accurate or inaccurate. If the observation of your experience is inaccurate, then you have failed to create your intention. If the observation of your experience is accurate, then you can start over, constantly and eternally engaging in this circular process of creation that is observable and inclusive. Everyone is ultimately the beneficiary or the victim of the accuracy of their own observations.

Etch this process into your mind. It is through this process that **you can create anything you intend.**

THE STRUCTURE OF GOD

If God is the projector and the projection of space, time, matter, and energy, then **God must be everything seen and unseen. While God may not be as traditional religions have depicted her, God can be understood and visualized.**

Does God have a long white beard? Does God float around in the sky? Is God a man? Is God a woman? How can God be observed, and how can he be inclusive? Is God a Hindu, a Buddhist, a Christian? To be all-inclusive, the umbrella of God has to cover everyone and every religion, even the atheist.

On a cloudless night, what do you see beyond the stars and moon? When you close your eyes, what do you see? When you shut your television off, what do you see?

You see a black void. It is no coincidence that the boundary of the universe is a black void in front of which everything unfolds. When you shut your eyes and cut off all light, you see a black void. Your television is black without any input but can broadcast any picture and story sent to it.

GOD IS THE BLACK VOID.

God is the black void from which everything flows, in the form of a hologram.

The black void projects the hologram. The theory that the universe is a hologram has been supported by scientific thought leaders such as Stephen Hawking and Leonard Susskind, an American physicist at the Stanford Institute for Theoretical Physics. What Hawking and Susskind haven't appreciated is the source of the hologram. The source is God.

The reason Hawking and Susskind have not recognized God as the source of the hologram is because scientists are limited to the rules that govern science, and those rules involve only that which can be calculated. Hawking and Susskind are distinguished scientists, but they are not artists, storytellers, philosophers, or poets. And this leaves their thought processes incomplete.

Before making the case for a holographic universe, let us first dismantle the concept that everything in the universe is physical. We'll do this by looking at scientific experiments that prove the physical universe is not actually physical at all.

But first, let us discuss basic scientific theory. Scientists make observations that lead to hypotheses, which are then tested. The results of the test are either measurable, predictable, and repeatable, or they are not. If an observation is measurable, predictable, and repeatable, the observation is accepted as a scientific fact. So, for something to be scientifically proven, there has to be a result that can be predicted and measured over and over again. The following amazing experiments have been scientifically proven:

1. the Heisenberg uncertainty principle
2. the existence of particles and antiparticles
3. the slit lamp experiment

These three observations demonstrate that the physical universe is not physical at all.

THE HEISENBERG UNCERTAINTY PRINCIPLE

All matter is constructed of particles, such as electrons and photons. To learn more about the universe, scientists measure these particles and study their speed. However, particles do something very strange when you try to study them. Bizarrely, the more precisely you try to measure the position of a particle, the more uncertain its velocity becomes; and the more precisely its velocity is calculated, the more uncertain its position becomes. So when you look at the smallest particles of matter, they run away. They do not want to be observed. Does this mean they are alive?

This phenomenon was first authenticated in the 1920s by Werner Karl Heisenberg, a German theoretical physicist, which is why it is called "the Heisenberg uncertainty principle."

Because of the uncertainty principle, scientists needed to procure other ways to study particles, so they began to look at the particle's quantum state. A particle's quantum state is its location and direction. Since scientists cannot pinpoint a particle's definite position or velocity, they look at the many positions that particles might occupy with the velocities the particles might possess. As a particle moves about, scientists track all of its possible positions and determine which of these is the most likely position. In order to determine this, the scientists treat particles as if they were waves.

The multitude of various positions that a particle can be in means that they appear as a series of continuous, oscillating waves. Imagine a piece of vibrating string. As it vibrates, the string arcs and dips through peaks and troughs. A particle also behaves like this, although its path is a series of overlapping waves, all happening at once. The likeliest position of the particle occurs in the arcs and the troughs where the waves correspond with each other, and the least likely positions are where the waves do not correspond. This pattern is known as interference, and it shows which positions and velocities are most probable for the particle's path.

THE EXISTENCE OF PARTICLES AND ANTIPARTICLES

In 1928, the physicist Paul Dirac made the stunning prediction that every fundamental particle in the universe has an antiparticle—the particle's identical twin, but with an opposite charge. Dirac predicted that when a particle and antiparticle met, they would be annihilated, releasing a poof of energy. Sure enough, the first antimatter particle—the positron, which is the electron's opposite—was discovered, and antimatter quickly became a part of the new science experiments, as well as popular culture.

What is extremely interesting about particles and antiparticles is that, once separated—either by large magnets or in a particle accelerator—the particle and the antiparticle will continue to travel in opposite but identical trajectories at 186,000 miles per second (also known as the speed of light), infinitely. Put another way, even apart and with no physical connection, the particle and its antiparticle continue to behave in a way that's dependent upon each other.

THE SLIT LAMP EXPERIMENT

The slit lamp experiment proves that the observer of an experiment influences the result of that experiment.

Photons being directed through a single slit will appear on a receptor as a single line, like bullets going through an opening. However, when you put two slits in front of the photons, they behave as a wave and make an interference pattern on the receptor. But as one observes the photons going through the two slits, they go back to acting like particles, making two different patterns on the receptor. The act of watching the photon makes it behave differently.

All of these experiments are repeatable and have, in fact, been repeated many times.

Furthermore, as if these three experiments are not enough, other experiments have revealed even more baffling and mysterious forces.

Consider the four fundamental forces in the universe: the electromagnetic force, the weak radioactive force, the strong nuclear force, and gravity. The most familiar is the **electromagnetic force**, which is what allows your cell phone and your microwave oven to work. This force is also what causes a magnet to stick to a refrigerator. The electromagnetic force is an inherent, unexplainable quality of the universe that manipulates electricity and magnetism in an undulating wave at different frequencies that can be dispersed and received through the universe infinitely in all directions at 186,000 miles per second. Although we take the electromagnetic force for granted, we do not understand where it comes from. We can manipulate the electromagnetic force, but we cannot create it.

The second force is the **weak nuclear force**, which acts on all particles that make up matter and which causes radioactivity. This weak interaction affects all the smallest particles, known as quarks. This nuclear force is "weak" because the particles that carry it can only exert force at short distances. However, at higher energies, the strength of the weak nuclear force increases until it matches that of the electromagnetic force. But even this "weak" force is not that weak, as it is also the force that initiates the nuclear fusion reaction that fuels the sun. It is a spontaneous and naturally occurring force that arises from "nothing."

The third force is the **strong nuclear force**, which binds protons and neutrons in the nucleus of an atom and binds the smaller quarks within the protons and neutrons. In contrast to the electromagnetic force and weak nuclear force, the strong nuclear force gets weaker at higher energies. At an exceedingly high energy, called "grand unification energy," electromagnetic force and weak nuclear force become stronger, while the strong nuclear force becomes weaker. At that point, all three forces reach equal strength and become distinct aspects of a single force—a force that might have played a role in the creation of the universe.

The final force of the universe is **gravity**. If you want to understand gravity, just hold out a beach towel and throw an orange in the middle of it. Then, drop a marble near the edge of the beach towel. The marble will roll toward the orange because the heavier orange is exerting a force on the surrounding towel. With gravity, a heavy object exerts a collapsing force on its neighboring space-time matrix, which may be made up of dark matter and dark energy. Dark matter and dark energy can be calculated, but they cannot be seen. Whether dark matter and dark energy exist or not, gravity does. The heavy object is warping something. It is causing smaller objects to flow toward it. We describe this as the heavy object warping the "fabric" of space-time around it.

In addition to the four mysterious forces of the universe, scientists have **string theory** to contemplate. Part of quantum physics, string theory states that as you go deeper and deeper into the workings of an atom, you see that there is nothing there—just energy waves resembling "strings" that oscillate in and out of existence. These energy waves are also known as quantum particles. Examples of quantum particles include quarks, electrons, and bosons. String theory helps explain the Heisenberg uncertainty principle, which detailed the elusiveness of these smallest "particles." Hence, they are not particles at all; they are waves of energy. Therefore, an atom is an invisible force field made of quantum particles, a kind of miniature tornado that emits waves of electrical energy.

So, what is the matter with the idea of the universe being physical? As it turns out, there is no such thing as matter—which in turn means that nothing in the universe is physical. The above experiments and descriptions of the forces of the universe make it clear that, all along, religions have been accurate about the spiritual makeup of the universe. Given the above objective, inclusive, measurable, and predictable observations, **there is nothing physical about the universe.** Given the above observations, **a holographic universe is the likely structure of everything seen and unseen.**

Even if you do not want to believe that the universe itself is a hologram, you must accept the fact that what you are visualizing right now is a hologram, because there is no light inside your skull. Light (photons) enters through the cornea of your eye and travels through the vitreous humor. Next, the photons reach the chemical receptors in the back of your eye, called "rods and cones," which feed and activate sodium and potassium channels, thus creating an electrical current along the optic nerve. The optic nerve, and this electrical current, then travels and crisscrosses through the center of your brain to the occipital lobe, which is ironically at the back of your head. The different electrical impulses are deciphered by the occipital lobe neurons and then "projected" for your viewing. This process also occurs while you dream, but without the photonic input. So, even if the universe is not a hologram, what you are witnessing in your occipital lobe is.

So, what does this have to do with God? And what does it have to do with the structure of God specifically?

The black void, which is God, projects the hologram. Based not only on religious dogma but also on scientific evidence, this is the most efficient way for a conscious, creative, eternal being to create the observable universe that we live in.

THE FUNCTION OF GOD

Observably, God's function is to create relativity, also known as relationship. In the black void, there is no relationship; everything is one, and everything is connected. There is no time. There is no space.

But in the universe, there are three dimensions: longitude, latitude, and height. Then there is also the fourth dimension of time. But even time is quirky and mysterious. In fact, time is relative.

Let us discuss Albert Einstein's theory of special relativity, which states that time itself is not fixed. **Time changes as speed changes.** Space and time are interwoven into a single continuum known as space-time. Events that occur at a certain time for one observer could occur at a different time for another. As Einstein worked out the equations for his general theory of relativity, he realized that massive objects caused a distortion in space-time. This distortion is the concept of gravity that we discussed previously. Like gravity, light also bends around a massive object, such as a black hole. This is referred to as special relativity. This means that the light can be used as a kind of lens for viewing things that lie behind a massive object. Astronomers routinely use this method to study stars and galaxies behind massive objects. They can observe the light bend. They can measure the differences in time from light as it bends around the large object.

Furthermore, this phenomenon shows that because the speed of light does not change for observers moving at different speeds, observers traveling relative to one another would calculate different times for the same event. For example, say a flash of light is projected out to two observers: one observer is traveling toward the light, while the other is traveling at greater speed in the opposite direction. For both observers, the speed of light would be the same, even though they are traveling at different speeds and going in different directions. This would mean that they each experience the flash event as if it happened at two contrasting times, because time is determined by the distance something has traveled divided by its speed. The speed of light is the same for both observers, but as the distance is different, the time is relative to each observer. If both observers carried clocks to record when the pulse of light was emitted, they would confirm two contrasting times for the same event. But who would be right? Neither observer. Time is relative and unique to both observers' perspectives.

Another way to understand this is that time slows down as you travel faster because momentum bends the fabric (probably dark matter and energy) of space-time, causing time to pass slower.

Hence, it follows that everything else is relative. There is up and down. There is now and then. There is big and small. There is fast and slow. There is young and old. There is here and there. There is day and night. **Most importantly, there is good and bad.**

3

LIFE

We are travelers on a cosmic journey—stardust swirling and dancing in the eddies and whirlpools of infinity. Life is eternal. But the expressions of life are ephemeral, momentary and transient.

The existence of ours is as transient as autumn clouds. To watch the birth and death of beings is like looking at the movements of a dance. A lifetime is like a flash of lightning in the sky, rushing by like a torrent down a steep mountain.

We have stopped for a moment to encounter each other, to meet, to love and to share. This is a precious moment, but it is transient. It is a little parenthesis in eternity. If we share with caring, lightheartedness, and love, we will create abundance and joy for each other. And then this moment will have been worthwhile.

—Deepak Chopra, The Seven Spiritual
Laws of Success, 1994

THE DEFINITION OF LIFE

Life is a spiritual journey in which we are guided forward by mysterious coincidences that are not coincidences at all but intended happenings. By connecting with the higher power that most people have come to call God, we can more readily recognize, speed up, and even create these intended happenings. Once one successfully does this, life will be experienced as a series of peak experiences, a cosmic billiard game with one shot always setting up the next. No longer will life be experienced as a ship being tossed about in a stormy sea. It will be experienced with the precision of a thread that goes through the eye of a needle and with the perfection of a newly formed snowflake.

THE PURPOSE OF LIFE

The purpose of life is to re-create yourself in the next greater and grander version of who you really are.
—Neale Donald Walsch

Re-creating yourself is unidirectional, always up, up, up!

Re-creating yourself is limitless. It does not necessarily refer to an objective part of your soul, mind, or body. Re-creating yourself does not necessarily pertain to your career, passion, hobby, or relationship. It can simply be your story.

Re-creating your story will be thoroughly discussed in an upcoming chapter.

Re-create yourself to wholeness, the whole of who you really are. And then keep re-creating over and over and over again.

This process never ends. And this is how we successfully deal with eternity.

THE STRUCTURE OF LIFE

Can you imagine spending an eternity with only one life to live?

This would be especially hard to imagine if that life was less than grand.

So, it follows that life is a circle. Souls renew themselves cyclically, achieving new and ever-expanding levels of spiritual evolution.

In the beginning of the journey, the agenda of the soul is survival. Once survival is mastered, then organizing and securing continued survival is next. When learning to organize and secure the survival, the challenge is creating not only that which sustains you but also that which you desire. Eventually, one will lose the desire to create for only oneself and gain the desire to create for others. Mother Teresa was such a soul. The only step after that, logically and observably, is to weave all prior agendas into one being. That is wholeness, which is living life fully. That is when you will experience the grandest version of the greatest vision you've ever held about who you are.

Again, can you imagine spending an eternity with only one life to live? I cannot.

THE FUNCTION OF LIFE

The function of life is spiritual growth—spiritual evolution, specifically. It is the journey of self-discovery in becoming who you really are in mind, body, and soul. That is, being whole and living life fully.

4

SOUL

You are not a drop in the ocean. You are the ocean in a drop.

—Rumi

THE DEFINITION OF THE SOUL

Each soul is a unique personage of God.

THE PURPOSE OF THE SOUL

The purpose of the human soul is to experience the highest feeling of love you can imagine.

THE STRUCTURE OF THE SOUL

The human soul can be observed as consisting of the following parts. These parts, when written out from top to bottom, form the shape of a pyramid.

Love

Truth Joy

Mind Body Soul

Sub Super Supra Conscious

Anger Fear Love Grief Envy

Taste Smell Hearing Touch Sight Intuition

Root Sacrum Gut Heart Throat Eye Crown

Let us start at the top. **Love, truth, and joy.** These can also be called empathy, awareness, and freedom. They crown the highest level of the pyramid structure of the human soul.

Mind, body, and soul follow these. The body experiences. The mind interprets incoming data and the experience, but the soul creates the experience. The soul is the witness. Feelings are the language of the soul. The purpose of the human soul is to experience the highest feeling of love you can imagine.

Next is the **subconscious, conscious, superconscious, and supraconscious**. The subconscious is that part of you that blinks and breathes without thought. The conscious is the part of which you are most aware, as it is the part that directly experiences your reality. The superconscious is that part of you that never left God, as it is also part of God's personality. It is how God is directly connected to everyone at all times. The superconscious is that voice in your head that speaks to you through feelings and thoughts. Finally, the supraconscious is all three parts working as one.

Sigmund Freud spoke of these parts of the personality as the id, the ego, and the superego. These describe the subconscious, conscious, superconscious, and supraconscious in the pyramid.

The next layer in the pyramid is the five emotions. As accepted by psychologists, **the five emotions are anger, envy, fear, grief, and love.**

Contrary to a widely held belief, anger can be good. Anger can be a way of saying, "No, I do not think so. That is not who I am." However, anger should never be permitted to turn into rage, as rage is dangerous.

Envy can also be good. Envy can be a way of saying, "I'd like to be more like that" or "That is admirable." Envy should never be permitted to turn into jealousy, as jealousy is dangerous.

Fear can be good. A healthy fear can help keep you alive. For example, it can keep you away from potentially harmful situations, such as standing on the edge of a cliff. Fear should never be permitted to turn into panic or paranoia, both of which are dangerous.

Grief can be good as well. Grief is an expression of love. I have personally delivered more than six thousand new lives, and I have seen heaps of joy at these births. But to this day, I am even more impressed with the love expressed through grief at funerals. Indeed, grief is love expressed. However, if left unchecked, grief can turn into suffering, sorrow, and sadness, which are all dangerous.

Love is good. Love cares and empathizes. Love nurtures and never harms. However, love should never turn into possession. To love something or someone is not to possess it. The desire to possess is dangerous.

After the emotions, **we have our six senses layered in the structure of this pyramid of the soul.** These include taste, smell, touch, hearing, vision, and, most importantly, intuition.

Finally, at the bottom of the pyramid, we have **the seven chakras.** At the bottom of the chakra body, we have the root chakra, which consists of sexuality and comedy. Above that, we have the sacral chakra, which consists of imagination and creativity. The sacral chakra is also useful in intimate relationships because imagination and creativity are useful in intimate relationships. Next is the gut chakra, which consists of determination and grit. Above that is the heart chakra, which consists of compassion and group concern. Above that is the throat chakra, which consists of eloquence and communication. Above that is the eye chakra, which consists of vision and intelligence. Finally, we have the crown chakra. The crown chakra consists of cosmic consciousness, awareness, and being awake.

To live fully, you must embrace every part of the human soul and use each as much as possible. Your mission, should you choose to accept it, is to imagine each part of the human soul as a dial that can be set anywhere from one to ten and to then turn each dial up to ten. This is your journey to wholeness. This is what will keep eternity exciting.

THE FUNCTION OF THE SOUL

The function of the human soul is to choose. At every juncture in your experience, you will have a choice. **At the root of every choice will be love or fear. Choose love—always and in all ways.**

5

DEATH

In My Father's house are many mansions: if it were not so, I would have not told you.

—Jesus

Death is a little tricky to observe. In religion, no one other than Jesus came back to tell us much about it. However, like religion, science has something to offer regarding information describing the process of death.

Dr. Eben Alexander is an American neurosurgeon and author. He wrote the book titled *Proof of Heaven: A Neurosurgeon's Journey into the Afterlife.*

I found his book to be one of the best scientific descriptions of death. He describes his experience during a medically induced coma for meningitis in 2008. For a detailed journey into his experience, I highly recommend reading his book.

Additionally, you may have heard of Elisabeth Kübler-Ross. She is a well-respected Swiss-American psychiatrist who studied the death and grief process of many dying patients. I recommend reading her book *On Death and Dying*. Her observations, along with Dr. Alexander's observations, reliably shed light on what to expect after we die.

Many other scientists and healthcare professionals have brought a scientific approach to the observation of death and dying, but I consider both Alexander and Kübler-Ross to be the best sources of this information.

The trajectory of their—as well as others'—observations regarding death can be interpolated and reconstructed. The following reconciles both religious and scientific accounts of death.

THE DEFINITION OF DEATH

The definition of death is the separation of your consciousness from your current reality and the realization that you still exist.

THE PURPOSE OF DEATH

The purpose of death is to *know* yourself and the grandest version of the greatest vision you hold about who you really are. Contrast this with the purpose of life, which is to *experience* yourself in the grandest version of the greatest vision you create. In life we *experience*; in death we *know*. The difference is not a subtle nuance. To *experience* something and to *know* something are quite different; this is the difference between life and death.

THE STRUCTURE OF DEATH

After realizing that you still exist, you will choose to stay in this current realm as long as it serves you. After accepting your death, you will move on to the **realm of belief**. This is where you experience everything in death exactly as you expected it to be. You will see the God of your choosing—God will show up in any form you believed He or She would. You will stay in the realm of belief until it no longer serves you, when you find a discrepancy between what you believe and what you desire.

When the two no longer match, as they frequently do not, you will move from the realm of belief to the **realm of desire**. All your desires will be fulfilled with effortless ease. When that serves you no longer, you will have the highest experience you will ever have—**a direct experiencing, recognizing of, and connecting with God**. Visually, you will see nothing but a black void. The feeling can best be explained as a shiver, only it's a shiver times one million. You will recognize this black void as God, your oldest eternal friend. You will remember God. There will be no experience in eternity that you will ever have like this.

After this experience, you will find yourself in a realm with souls that vibrate at your frequency. In this realm, you will re-examine your past life. You will reexamine the things you did well and your creations that worked. You will reexamine all the things you wish you could redo—your creations that did not work. From there, you will begin to create your **birth vision**.

Your birth vision consists of what your next life is going to be. My advice here is to pick a life that will challenge you but that is attainable. If you pick your next life and it is too easy, there will be no evolution of your soul. If you create a birth vision that is too difficult, the results may not be what you want. **The goal is to get you to experience your next best self, one step at a time.** Every sequence in reincarnation and every building block of the soul has a purpose, and the direction is always up. The direction is always to someplace freer, more joyful, and more deeply entrenched with love.

Next, you are born. (And hopefully your parents have picked out a good obstetrician to see over your safe arrival.)

THE FUNCTION OF DEATH

The imagining and creation of your next life, while building your whole self throughout your eternal journey, keeps you and God from getting bored.

It is in the place we have come to call "death" that the boredom of eternity is eradicated. **This is death's function.**

And the information provided in this book has just come full circle.

6

PLAN

Two roads diverged in a wood, and I—
I took the one less traveled by,
And that has made all the difference.

—Robert Frost

So, now what?

Hopefully, at this point, the information in this book resonates with you. More importantly, I hope it resonates with your observations. I hope the information in this book provides a framework to help you navigate away from any anxiety, confusion, and lack of joy, and navigate into deeper meaning and happiness.

All the parts of the preceding observations are compact and critical. But there are a couple of "levers" you may want to keep your hands on.

First, always go back to the definition of life as a spiritual journey on which we are led forward by "coincidences" that are not coincidences at all but are intended happenings. Connect with God through meditation, thought, and self-reflection to help identify, speed up, and even create these happenings.

Next, use the purpose of God to create your forthcoming intentions. Become familiar with using the wheel of intention, perspective, thought, word, action, experience, and observation. This will turn you into a creating machine.

Then, never forget your soul's function: at every juncture in your experience, you will always have the choice between love and fear. Always choose love. **Observe what is so, and do what works. Love works.**

Finally, go back to the structure of your soul. Remember that your soul has many parts. Individually evolving each one of those parts to a higher and more grand state of being is how you will eventually unveil your true, whole self to yourself and to others.

Since the infinite, intelligent, and eternal creative energy of the universe that most people have come to call God was smart enough to create reincarnation, you can reincarnate after you have become your whole self as many times as it serves you.

Eventually, you'll start over again from the beginning, as a young soul, and this cycle will continue for eternity. Each cycle will be like a wave in the ocean; from a distance, they will look similar, but none will be the same. There is no end to the cycle. **There is no end to God.** The ideas, characters, creations, and stories will never stop flowing to you through the vastness of the void.

It is this cycle that prevents any one of us, including God, from getting bored with eternity. **Eternity is no longer God's dilemma but God's blessing.**

7

STORY

All the world's a stage,
And all the men and women merely players;
They have their exits and their entrances,
And one man in his time plays many parts.

—William Shakespeare

Without our stories, we are nothing but animals. None of the previous observations in this book have any value without the stories of our lives and their entangled characters. Without stories, we as individuals, and we as civilizations, are nothing.

Whether you believe that authoring the story of your life is something you do now or something you have done before you were born matters not.

I believe that before we are born, we create a birth vision.

When I was a young boy, my oldest sister explained that an angel placed their finger on my lips to keep God a secret—that was her explanation of the philtrum above anyone's upper lip. I think this may be symbolically accurate.

Regardless, every story, whether it is your life, a book, a television series, or a movie, has structure. In this chapter, that structure will be outlined observationally. The following structure applies not only to fiction writing but also to the writing of your birth vision.

Every relevant story starts with a question: What if?

What if I was born an alcoholic and went to work at a brewery?

What if I was a warrior who lived in the time of dragons?

What if I was born gay in a religiously conservative family?

What is your "What if"? Every life lived has one. It is the beginning of the birth vision. Everyone's "what if" is chosen and created by each soul individually.

Then, there is "window dressing." This is a technique used to attract the reader, the observer, into the story. For example, perhaps a story begins with a gory emergency C-section from which the infant nearly dies and ends up spending months in the neonatal intensive care unit, much like my own arrival. That would attract the reader.

After the window dressing, characters are introduced and developed. The observer becomes familiar with the personalities of the characters. Then conflict occurs. Then plot builds around conflict. The plot plays out in accordance with the personalities of the characters. Then there is the climax. The climax should be character driven, not plot driven. The author should not style the ending as he or she wishes. Instead, the personalities of the characters should seed the climax. **Finally, all good endings should be unpredictable but inevitable.** No one should be able to guess the ending, but everyone should be able to understand why the story had to end the way it did.

This is the blueprint of all stories.

When creating your birth vision, do not choose a story that's too difficult. Do not choose a story that's too easy. If you pick a life that's too difficult, it may not have the result you intend. Pick a life that's too easy and there will be little or no spiritual evolution.

Do not choose too narrowly. Remember the distinct parts of the human soul and try to choose lives that evolve all of them.

The definition, purpose, structure, and function of God, life, soul, and death are all to serve a workable process and framework in the story of our lives. They give your life meaning. They give your life direction. And they bring you joy, awareness, and love eternally.

8

VOID

And God said. Let us make man in our image and after our
likeness: and let them have dominion...

So God created man in his own image, in the image of
God created male and female.

—Genesis 1:26-27

Computer screens and television screens are black for one reason: it is from the blackness that anything can be created.
The black vastness of outer space and the darkness
behind your own eyelids have one thing in common: they both look
like a void. It is no coincidence that when people faint, they black
out. Through meditation or other life experiences, it is possible for
anyone to experience this void.

This is not a new concept.

This is the *sunyata* in the Buddhist philosophy. This is the *brahman* in the Upanishads, sacred Hindu writings. And this is *Wuji* in
Taoism. This is the "I am that I am" in Judeo-Christian tradition.

All describe a primordial yet undifferentiated void that births all realities.

It was a chilly November night when my mother and sister took me, around age fourteen, to North County in St. Louis, Missouri, to pick up my aunt Nina. Aunt Nina suffered from advanced arthritis. My mother, at that time, had recently been diagnosed with a laryngeal tumor. My sister suffered from agoraphobia and panic attacks.

We were a Catholic family who went to church on Sundays and should have gone to confession more often. We were not the most religious family, but we did believe in God, Jesus, and the power of prayer.

Our mission on this night was to visit a nondenominational Christian preacher in North County. His name was Brother Dennis Goodell, and he was from California. He had a reputation for being able to heal with his hands.

We were beyond skeptical.

He had rented a small, empty space in a strip mall and filled it with folding chairs, a microphone, and, on this night, people. Upon entering, I could hear him, as well as others, praying loudly and passionately. I had no experience with evangelical preachers, Pentecostal preachers, or Baptist ministers. He had been all three. This was a new experience for me.

During the service, he introduced himself and explained that healing occurs from within us as we connect with God. He did not claim to have any healing powers himself, but he said he acted more as a conduit for "sacred energy."

He approached Aunt Nina and told her she had arthritis. This was obvious by looking at her hands and seeing the large knuckles with sausage fingers. He laid his hands on Aunt Nina, and she fell backward into the hands of two complete strangers. She lay on the ground for quite a while. My mother and sister were shocked but accepting of Aunt Nina lying on the floor unconscious.

After revealing further insight into others' health conditions and emotional dilemmas, Brother Goodell accurately assigned anxiety and panic to my sister. I thought to myself that this could easily be spotted by an accurate observer from an individual's body language.

I was a little more taken aback when he approached my mother. Somehow, he knew she had a tumor, though he couldn't tell what kind. The fact he knew about the tumor impressed me simply because there was no way he could have known. He told her that the tumor was benign, but he laid his hands on her anyway. She fell back into the strangers' arms and lay on the ground for several minutes. We found out several weeks later, after my mother's surgery, that her tumor had been benign. It was actually a laryngeal polyp.

My interest was piqued. Still skeptical, I did not know quite what to expect when he welcomed everyone in the audience to the stage just prior to ending the service. With curiosity, I approached. He asked me my name and religion, and I told him. He jokingly told me that God loves Catholics too. He asked me if I believed in God and if I wanted to be blessed. I responded with a simple "yes." What happened next was life changing.

I found myself suspended in a pitch-black void. It was familiar. It was observing me. It was alive. **It was God.** The feeling I had can be explained as the chill that runs down your spine when you are unexpectedly excited, only it was much stronger (multiply the ordinary chill by an infinite number). I woke up on the ground, with the two strangers above me asking me if I was okay. Tears of exhilaration filled my eyes as I understood exactly what had happened. I knew I had just seen *behind the curtain*.

This book is based on observation, not revelation, so while you may not believe my experience in the void, not disclosing this experience would leave this book incomplete.

We have already discussed how thought leaders such as Leonard Susskind and Stephen Hawking have endorsed ultimate reality as a hologram. The nature of the universe as a hologram is now currently taught in most colleges and universities. This theory is starting to be accepted alongside other theories, such as the general theory of relativity and the big bang.

In a recent interview, Leonard Susskind stated that the universe is like a bubble created by the hologram, with everything that has happened and ever will happen imprinted on the edges of the universe. He does not know if the hologram is being projected inward from the edges, but it seems that way. When asked what we can expect to be revealed about this hologram in the future, he simply said, "Surprises."

I am bold enough to say that one of the surprises will be that **the hologram projects from an inward to outward direction**. It is *not* projecting from the edge of the universe inward but from the inside outward. I believe this to be so because, as I have explained using the slit lamp experiment, the observer influences that which is observed. Therefore, because we affect that which is external, it is more likely that the source of the hologram is projected from us, not onto us.

Furthermore, if indeed the universe is a hologram, then a theory reconciling Newtonian physics with quantum physics is futile. It would be like trying to determine the weight of a tree in a cartoon. That is why it is mathematically impossible to create an equation or a theory of everything encompassing both Newtonian physics and quantum physics.

This begs the question: **What is the source of the hologram?** The source of the hologram is the void I experienced that chilly November night in North County, St. Louis. Each one of us collectively projects the universe. We are the authors of our own stories. We are all different personalities of the same energy that most people call God. And you are now privy to what God is up to via the all-inclusive and objective observations detailed in this book, *Behind the Curtain*.

ABOUT THE AUTHOR

Frank Patrick is an obstetrician and gynecologist in St. Louis, Missouri, his hometown. He attended the University of Missouri–Kansas City Medical School. He has five siblings and lives with his wife Amy and stepson Jackson near St. Louis Missouri. Dr. Patrick enjoys playing ice hockey, biking, and snow skiing. His favorite sports team is the St. Louis Blues hockey team. His favorite movie is *What Dreams May Come*. His favorite song is *My Sweet Lord* by George Harrison. His favorite author is Neale Donald Walsch. His favorite vacation destination is Siesta Key, Florida. Dr. Patrick's mantra is "We are all the beneficiaries and/or the victims of the accuracy of our own observations." His favorite angel is Saint Michael.